conversations after sunset

Reverend Henry C. Frascadore

Copyright

First Edition
Published and distributed in the United States by
BeyondtheWeepingWillowTree.org
ISBN: 978-0-615-85141-9

ALSO BY REVEREND HENRY C. FRASCADORE

Beyond the Weeping Willow Tree

. . . Mystery is a Gift Wrapped in Ordinary Paper

Acknowledgements

The more deeply I enter into the process of writing, the more I realize that the publication of a book like this, far from being a solo venture, is possible only with the collaboration of countless others. And so I would like to express my gratitude to friends past and present who directly contributed to my work in so many ways, great and small: in preparing the text for publication, notably Steve Goddard, Gerri Naples and Natalie Pucci; in reading the manuscript and in making suggestions, especially Sharon Ayotte, Sr. Corby Coperthwaite, CoS, Leeanne Frisina, Christine Looby, Jackie Marenholtz, Mary Anne Plourde, Sr. Maureen Reardon, RSM.

Finally, my thinking and writing throughout my years of ministry have been enriched by longtime friends, including the late Rev. Thomas Stack, Rev. Henry P. Cody, and Sr. Maris Stella Hickey, CSJ, to all of whom I owe an ongoing debt of gratitude. And most of all, a special thank-you to Archbishop Henry Mansell of the Archdiocese of Hartford, without whose blessing and encouragement I never would have undertaken such a project in the first place.

To all those whose contributions have made this book a reality, a sincere thank-you.

Rev. Henry C. Frascadore

Introduction

Some may find it quirky that Father Henry Frascadore's world includes animals that communicate with one another, flowers that tell us how to live, the moon as an artistic burglar, pets talking with their masters, as well as lessons from scriptures and vignettes of Jesus healing lepers and feeding the needy. But to the Hartford author of this unforgettable poetry collection, it just comes naturally, for these are all creations of God.

Henry, as the retired Catholic priest likes to be called, lives across the street from downtown's Bushnell Park, where he and his black lab Ramsey walk several times a day, rubbing elbows with 150-year-old elms, a fish-stocked pond, and the homeless people who have become their friends. Along the way, Henry shares lessons with his readers, such as an appeal to slow down if we want to fully perceive and savor the blessed world around us.

Steve Goddard

Steve Goddard is a Hartford attorney, author, historian and book critic.

Table of Contents

à chacun son goût

on our walk through the park this morning
i asked Ramsey
why do you sniff trees
he countered
why do you stare at trees
then in perfect French he added
à chacun son goût

the almost full moon

the almost full moon
sneaked into my house
through the blinds of my window
at two-thirty this morning
it drew yellow lines
on my bedroom wall
and wrapped the
bookcase and closet
in yellow ribbons

ancient English Elm

today dawn showed me a sketch
she did of the ancient English Elm
that stands by the side of the pond

she sketched it upside down
on the still black water
but wouldn't let me buy it

it was part of the pond's
permanent gallery
and not for sale she said

the brass Airedales

Along with the "scugnizzi" and my grandfather's Bible
On top of my bookcase beside my chair
Are two Airedale bookends made of heavy brass.
They have been with me since my childhood.
I remember them clearly sitting on the table next to our
        living room couch.
They held up my childhood books.
They couldn't read the books but heard them read enough
        to know their stories.
Those and a picture of my mother as a very young girl
Are the only two things I have from the house I grew up in.

Our family dog, Jerry, was an Airedale.
He fought all the time with the Husky next door.
And he rolled in cow manure.
I wonder why I loved him so much.

But I did and made believe that the Airedales guarding the
        books
Would tell Jerry
To stop fighting with Mr. West's dog
And rolling in the manure of Mr. Rossini's cows.

But they didn't listen to me. I suspect that they told Jerry
To keep doing the things he enjoyed doing,
Subscribing to their rule "do what is fun" and
When it stops being fun, then and only then, stop doing it.

If for no reason other than that,
I'll keep them by my side
And give them to someone I love
Before I die.

a car alarm is blasting away

a car alarm is blasting away on Gold Street
everyone hears it
but thinks that someone else will take care of it

an elephant cries
when its ivory tusks
are cut for a statue's eyes
a tree cries when felled
fearing that the mountainside
will soon be barren
a child cries
but its eyes are dry
as dry as its mother's breasts

everyone hears them crying
but thinks someone else will take care of it

children are the greatest

the disciples seem to have spent
more time wondering about the future
their future in particular
than they did about the present

recently Jesus heard them squabbling
about who among them was going
to be the greatest in the kingdom
as though Jesus was going to give them
grades when the kingdom came

and pass out awards
like thrones horses and servants
based on their speaking ability
or organizational skills

today they're squabbling again
about rank and Jesus tells them
to look and listen to a child
and get the answer
they are looking for

children are always asking questions
and their questions are about the here and now
they are curious about the world
they are living in

they aren't interested in what's ahead
they are curious about what's right
in front of their noses
the immediate is what is important

after the eight-thirty mass today
a three-year-old child
named Jacob asked me
why the leaves are changing colors

not having a "goggle mind"
i told him that the trees wanted
to show us that green
wasn't the only color in their wardrobe

he wasn't satisfied with my answer
neither was his
older sister
i didn't blame them

but that's not the point
--children are interested in the
"evolving now" for that's the work of saints
that's why children are the greatest in heaven

conversations after sunset

i regret that there
wasn't a stenographer
traveling along with the disciples that
followed Jesus through Palestine
if there were
he could have sat with them
in the evening and recorded what they talked about
after Jesus went to sleep

last week for example
after Jesus told them
during the day
the things they didn't want to hear
things about his eventual
murder upon a cross
the followers stayed up all night
talking more about how his death
would end their dreams
of a kingdom with thrones robes and banquet halls
than they did about his forecast
of a brutal crucifixion

the stenographer wouldn't have missed
the thread of selfishness
running through their conversations
and faithfully recorded his observations
in his manuscript

and this week
after the sun had set
the disciples
started squabbling over
who was the closest to Jesus
the most qualified for leadership
the best preacher

that evening's conversation around the fire
would have kept the stenographer's pen going for hours
he was stunned by
how narrow-minded they were
as they talked about one another's
faults and failings
and to make matters worse
their bickering continued over breakfast

but this time
Jesus overheard them
and called them on their pettiness
he told them that if they wished
to make something of themselves
they had to stop focusing on themselves
and look carefully
at the child playing in the yard with his friends
he said
"there is your model of greatness
curious and full of energy
anxious to get on with life
but you are still stuck on yourselves
still thinking more of getting than giving
wake up
for it is into empty hands
that gifts are given"

i woke up this morning
still regretting that there wasn't
a stenographer who
sat with the disciples
every night for three years
recording their thoughts
and conversations

for if there had been
i am sure that we would find
in his writing overwhelming evidence
of Jesus' patience love and forgiveness
for those he chose to carry on his work

and if Jesus could forgive the pettiness
of those who had the privilege of his daily company
how much more ready is he to forgive us
our foolishness greed jealousy and ignorance
we who have never had the chance to
hear his voice
look into his eyes
or feel the touch of his hand

yes while i regret that there is no
evidence of a stenographer
i still hope
that someday I'll wake up
and read that an adventurer
seeking shelter from the
hot Palestinian sun
entered a cave on the hillside
above the dead sea
and found inside a leather bound
manuscript entitled
"conversations after sunset"

the cuff of shame

in Jesus' time a man with a withered hand
couldn't eat in the company of friends
he was shunned by those
who could use both hands

so when Jesus saw him in the shadows
of the synagogue
he called him to the front of the room
and before all present he healed him

the scribes condemned Jesus' healing
for it was performed on the sabbath
a day reserved for lifesaving work
and a twisted hand didn't qualify

Jesus didn't see it that way
one second of groundless shame
was time too long
to deny another the fullness of life

stretch out your hand
he said
and raise it high above the heads of those
who came to pray

and let them see that with your hand made new
the rule of sabbath had to be broken
to set you free
from the cuff of baseless shame

people's ways of speaking and acting and thinking
have changed greatly
since the time of Jesus
but his message of compassion

and his desire
to free each and every person
from one second of
needless shame is as strong now as then
and as his disciples today
his kindness and compassion
are to be reflected in everything
we say and do

often we meet people
who live with a shame imposed
upon them by society or self-inflicted

they blame themselves
for failed marriages

for failing to achieve the expectations
set for them by others

for lacking the courage
to admit their true feelings

like Jesus we are to free them from groundless shame
by trusting in their good conscience and
respecting the difficult decisions they have had to make
assuring them that we understand

Jesus knew what he had to do
that day in the synagogue
he acted without delay
knowing that one second of needless shame
is a second too long to endure

it would be contrary to
the teachings of Jesus

if we were to turn away
from those who need us most
and a disavowel
of the name we bear

a duck and a limb

the first sad note

another duckling is missing
first there were five then four then three then two
today just one

the mother duck was keeping
her last close to her side
and the father was on "hawk watch"

the second sad note

the turkey oak which has been
standing by the carousel
for a hundred and fifty years

and a favorite of mine
had a large limb
amputated yesterday

ducklings and a limb
things i never thought
i'd miss four years ago

but once i began
looking at things
more carefully

i find that there
are more things
i miss

Easter

early this morning
through the thin branches
of a tall bald cypress tree
i saw the half moon
crossing the southern sky
and heard a small bird
singing from somewhere high above it
i rejoiced that today
started this way

everlasting beauty

The park after Memorial Day was a mess.
Plastic cups and soda cans floated on the surface of the
pond.
And potato chip bags and crushed napkins were left by the
benches.

The day itself was beautiful.
The warm sunlight spread across the lawns,
and the sounds of fun were easily heard everywhere.

Why is it that ugliness and beauty often converge?
The temptation is to focus on the ugliness
and concede defeat.

To make the Styrofoam cups and crumpled napkins
the center of our attention is to pay homage
to the irreverent people who insulted the earth.

The better part would be to raise our eyes and
contemplate
the architecture of the oak and elm trees
and know earth's beauty will endure despite everything.

every morning i get up

every morning i get up
make coffee
sit in my brown leather chair
read the psalms

take my dog for a walk in the park
keep my journal
have breakfast
then decide what i want to write about

this morning i had trouble deciding
because
everywhere i looked in my room
there was something with something to say

the bronze statue of the neapolitan street boy
my grandfather's Bible
the painting of the solitary fisherman
and favourite bookends

the street boy told me
that he was a gift to me from my father
who in nineteen forty-five had just returned from
his first visit to the country he had left when he was
seventeen

the Bible is old and very worn
and it told me that my grandfather read from it
each morning and again before bedtime
silently with head bowed

and translated its passages
into gentle deeds and simple needs
proving to be more persuasive
than sermons

i get up and move around
pour another cup of coffee
talk to the dog
look out the window

think about what I am going to have for lunch
turn on the dishwasher
and the clothes dryer
return a phone call or two

and then i get back to work
and listen to what
the solitary fisherman
has to say this morning

he keeps telling me to
keep things simple
say what i have to say
and be brief

what i like about the fisherman
is that he is calm and self-possessed
even though the clouds in the
background are thickening

nothing is bothering him
he has work to do
and he is doing
what he has chosen to do

and while he appears to be alone
he knows that when he gets back to shore
there will be those who will help him
unload the boat and enjoy the evening

ah the bookends
near me are two brass Airedales
that have been with me for
seventy-nine years

one of my clearest memories
of childhood is these two dogs
never needing to be fed
or taken for a long walk

i would talk to them as though they understood
what i was saying
i can shut my eyes and see them
on the table near the couch

what they told me this morning
is that they wished they could have read
all the books that they held
through all these years

especially the ones about
airedales and retrievers and chows
and compare notes
about the things that made them the happiest

we wouldn't be surprised to learn
that loving and being loved
would be right up there
with being scratched under the chin

flowers tell us how to live

into Bushnell Park
through the entrance off Wells Street
are plots of crocuses
breaking through
the winter's hard ground
with stiff yellow fingers

crocuses aren't afraid
to take their chances
crusty snow
can't stop
their prophesying--
        buck up
        spring is near

into Elizabeth Park
by the road off steele
i find a place to stop
near the trellises
where the prickled vines
are neatly tied
waiting patiently for ground to soften
and sun to blaze
        assuring admiration
        for their roses' blooming

flowers tell us ways to live
by listening with our eyes

fourteen cherry trees

fourteen cherry trees line the walkway
from the street to the pond in the park
i hadn't looked at them carefully
until this morning
i had other things on my mind
new cushions for the balcony
the Zen master wrote
"Oh wondrous marvel:
I chop wood
I draw water from the well"
wood is still wood
water is still water
all that changes
is the way they are seen
this morning i saw
them as cherry trees

freedom delayed is denied

i was concerned about a
        yellow shopping bag caught on a twig
                in a bush alongside jewell street
in the morning wind
        it thrashed madly
                attempting to break free
i had been watching it
        for two days
                so this morning
i decided to
        set it free
                but by the time
i got to it
        it had been freed
                by a man more compassionate than i

friendship

Word spread quickly in small Galilean towns
Jesus was in one of them today and everyone knew it in
 minutes
The close friends of a paralytic
wanted to take him to Jesus for curing
They had been used to taking him with them
wherever they went
He grew up with them
They rarely left him alone
Certainly they weren't going to miss this chance
of getting him as fast as they could
to the feet of the man known as the "miracle worker"
They put him on his pallet
as they had so many times before
and carried him to the house where Jesus was
They couldn't get in
The house was packed with people
who too had come to see Jesus
The paralytic's friends had to think fast
Without asking the owner's permission
they climbed up onto his rooftop and
spread the slats that kept the rain out
and through the wide opening lowered
their friend to Jesus' feet

Here
at least for me
the strangest thing happens

Before even going to the pallet
to speak to the paralytic
Jesus speaks directly to his friends
and tells them that their faith
has won them forgiveness
Amazing

Amazing
Their lifelong care for their friend
Their ingenuity under pressure
Their enduring love for him
was more than enough to immediately
earn the forgiveness of their sins from Jesus

frustration versus trust

Peter was frustrated.
He had been fishing all night
    and hadn't caught a thing.
He had been through this before.
He should have taken it in stride.
But that's not the way it goes with fishermen.
They go out each night thinking
    that this is the night
    they'll haul in more fish than they can count.

On the shore was Jesus.
He could see Peter and his crew.
When the boat got close enough to shore
    he invited himself aboard.
Peter didn't object.
Jesus climbed on and sat near the front of the boat.
He knew Peter's frustration
    so without being asked for an opinion
    Jesus told Peter to throw the nets in again for
        another try.
Peter snapped back, "We've been doing that
    all night with no success."
Jesus told him to try again.
On the say-so of Jesus
    Peter threw the nets overboard
    and within minutes they were full of fish.
When Peter got home that night
    and told his wife about the day he had,
    she told him that the miracle wasn't
    the net full of fish
    but the weakness of frustration
    in the face of trust.

the full moon

The full moon last night
was bright and proud of itself.
It was what it wanted to be:
provocative and romantic.
It knew that there
were people on earth who were waiting
to see it full: lovers anxious to hold hands
and writers depending
upon it to start them thinking.
And it was determined not
to disappoint them.
And it didn't.

But in a day or two
it knew it would be time to start waning again.
It would have
a couple of weeks
of peace and quiet
to work on three love songs
which it will run by two of its closest stars
Algorab and Gienah
and a story line
it plans to ask Jupiter about
being the critic that it is.
In the meantime it is keeping
the melody and plots
under lock and key
being confident
that all will be ready for the lovers
and the writers
a month from now
when it has waxed perfectly.

gave all she had

She thought that no one was watching
        when she dropped two small coins
        in the basket
But she was mistaken
Jesus saw her
        and made her a true
        heroine
It was not the amount she gave
        that had mattered
        it was her thoughtfulness
for the slightest bit of goodness
        is enough to sustain
        another through
        a day of awfulness

get a dog and have saintly thoughts

One of the advantages of having a dog is
he gets me out of the house by six
six in the morning that is
He likes the early morning
He has the park to himself
He can sniff each post and bush without the interference of
other dogs
And it's quiet
few
if any
buses and their hissing brakes at stop lights
Moreover I let him off his leash
He can run free from the pump house to the carousel with
no restraint
He thinks he's in heaven
especially when the sky is clear
and the moon is high
as it was this morning
sided by Jupiter with its sidekick star Aldebaran
On my own for a few minutes
I think I am in heaven too
It is a time to walk slowly and think peacefully
And frankly
it is easier to agree with the scriptures
I had read before leaving
This morning Paul in his letter is telling his people in
Phillipi not to
put themselves before others
vainglory and selfishness
are stumbling blocks on the way to holiness
There is no doubt about it
if you wish to think of yourself in a saintly fashion
get a dog and walk early every morning
before the phone rings

get up and get going

I am stunned by Jesus
in the way he says things.
You are forgiven
so now get up and go home.
He is so matter of fact.
You've been on the mat for years
wondering what you would do
if you had the chance.
Well I am telling you now
you have the chance
to make the dreams you've been having
for years come true.
No longer do you have an excuse
saying that if you could you would.
Now you can
so do it.

It's not a mat
that confines you.
What's the difference between
a mat and laziness?
Probably none.
Jesus says to us
get up and go home.
Snap out of it.
Do the things you have been dreaming about doing.
If you haven't been dreaming
about something to do
that's most likely what
you should be doing.

harp and lyre

on leaving the house
i look up

to see if the sun is high enough
to color the eastern sky timid red

and if Venus has yet
to step out on stage

the psalmists early in the morning
thanked God with harp and lyre

for granting them
another day

certainly more entertaining instruments than
computer keys

but to the ears of God
who hears what others miss

the dull beat of cs ks and bs
is music to forgiving ears

and while we might wish
to hear again the

melodies of praise and gratitude
as strummed in King David's time

an appreciative God thoroughly enjoys
whatever instruments are used

at day's beginning to announce
our thanks for another day of sun

harvesting mussels

Hanging on the wall
opposite my bookcase
is a watercolor painting of a
man standing alone in a flat bottomed rowboat
harvesting mussels.

He's been doing this since he was a kid.
You can tell just by looking at him.
He knows what he's doing.
He's focused and determined.

He learned harvesting from his father--
get up early
before the sun rises,
stake out your territory,
find a spot where the sea is calm
and close to shore.

Then let the sea tell you what to do.
Listen carefully to the water,
his father told him,
pay attention to its mixed sounds,
memorize every one of them.
Together they'll reveal what you must do
to harvest well.

I loved being with you

On the last day of his earthliness
Jesus said to his friends,
"I loved being with you--
working, praying, laughing, and crying.

I loved you from the first moment we met:
the way you accepted me
with no questions asked
and followed me wherever I went.

But now it is time to go.
I have done what I was sent to do.
Now it is up to you, so go, knowing that I will be with you.
I will never leave you.

I'll be at your side
to fill your glass
with extraordinary wine
when your spirits run dry.

I'll still the stormy sea
when its waves
threaten to dump
your dreams overboard.

I'll open your
ears to hear the song of a bird
when the allure of creation
starts to fade.

I'll say 'arise'
when you've fallen so many times
you think you
will never stand again.

I'll sit at your table
when the one you love most
passes through the door of death,
to remind you that life is always in the present tense.

I'll be there when your earthliness ends
to tell you
how happy you have made me
by matching your footsteps to mine."

if dogs could talk

rams and i always walk side by side.
he never fights the leash.
well, almost never.
little dogs and squirrels urge him to tug for freedom.

i talk while we walk.
i'll ask him to listen to the birds,
and to look at the gleam on the Capitol's dome,
or give me his opinion on the weather or
on the loud groans of the buses pulling up Gold Street.

and occasionally i'll ask if he has any thoughts on
scripture.
today i asked him about Isaiah's canticle and
did he agree with him that we waste the earth.
i am always looking for new ideas
and i don't care where they come from.

but this is the point.
i do the talking.
he never says a word.
he keeps everything to himself.
it drives me crazy.
i wish he'd speak once in a while.
but no, never a word.

on the other hand
maybe it's best that he keep
his opinions to himself
or, as Andy Rooney once said,
if dogs could talk,
we'd get rid of them.

inconsequential things

i remember inconsequential things
one morning while visiting
my high school friend mac
at cornfield point back in the late forties
i overheard his sister ellen
ask her friend lorraine if she were taking her
toothbrush on their vacation together the following week
lorraine said yes
ellen said good
then i don't have to take mine
why after all the things that mac and i did at
the beach that year
do i remember that

it's not the gondola rides
nor the side street restaurants
nor the tour of the duomo
that i remember from my trip to venice
fifty years ago
but the seven dollar (4500 lira) gelato
i bought in the galleria on a friday afternoon
why from the mound of art and architecture i saw
do i remember the cost
of a dish of ice cream

and i wonder if trees
remember strange things
given the hundreds of years
they live and the myriad of events
that have gone on around them
during that time

i thought of this one morning while
walking by the stump of an old sweet gum tree
that had just been cut down

if i had had the chance to get into
the mind of the tree and ask it to recall
something from the time
it stood and watched the Memorial Arch being built
in eighteen eighty-five
it probably would say something as inconsequential as
"the whinny of a dray horse in the middle of the night
that nearly scared the life out of me"

Isaiah 44:15

The Lord said
I have carved you on the palm of my hand
I read that and immediately looked
at my palm
And sure enough I saw the carved
lines going every which way
Some curved
others straight
Some long
others short
And they crisscross
one another
stop abruptly
then continue on down to my wrist
The Lord's carvings resemble the
twists and turns of my daily life
When I awake I never know what's in store
Things that I think predictable
change suddenly
And I have to be ready for the
quick turnaround
But
and this is an important *but*
The Lord is right there
ready to help me handle the sudden
turn of events--
the sharp corners
the abrupt stops
that's if I trust in his ever-presence
And the more I studied the palm of my hand
I began to see in it
the story of my life
There are no predictable roadways
no assurances that there won't be bumps in the way
The only predictable thing is that

if I hold my hand steady
and cup it
my fingers bend upwards
letting me know that
The Lord is there ready to catch me
at the end of the journey

it is all in the gait

It is all in the gait.
Short, slow steps.
No need to rush anymore.
Those days are over.
Walk attentively
taking nothing for granted.

Attend to all that
you had missed the first time through:
the ground beneath you,
the air that wraps around you,
the sky that covers you,
and the colours that please you.

Listen, feel and look
at everything carefully.

Rushing to be first is a hoax.
In the rush
the gold is missed,
as the kisses are missed
and the myths are missed
and the reds, yellows and greens, too.

it's the gait that matters

A robin sitting on a spruce branch reminded me to linger.
He sat on the branch
taking his time
to look around
and take in the view.

Ramsey too teaches me to linger.
He goes from shrub to tree trunk
carefully smelling their roots and leaves.
It appears that he is taking
notes on the variety of scents.

From the robin and the dog
I have learned to linger
and appreciate the inexhaustible offerings
of nature.

Lingering is a matter of gait.
It doesn't mean stopping.
It means slowing down,
changing the pace and spread of steps,
and paying attention to what is beside me,
below and above me.

If I walk quickly, I miss things.
If I take big and hurried steps
I miss the shape of a leaf I hadn't noticed before,
the odd contortions of a sycamore's branches,
and the rhythm of the fountain's falling water.

The gait of my morning walk sets my day
off on, if you pardon the pun, the right foot.
I have time to think about things,
things that I never took the time to think about.

I spent the first years of my life walking fast.
I was always in a hurry to get somewhere
before others got there.
I made the mistake of thinking
that being first was the ultimate prize.

Now I know differently.
It's the gait that matters.

Jesus antagonized his friends

Jesus tells Peter things he doesn't want to hear
Peter didn't want to hear Jesus talk about being
humiliated and spat upon
tortured and beaten
stripped naked and murdered on a cross
and Peter wasn't alone
none of the disciples wanted to hear Jesus talk about
being killed
they preferred it when he talked about a future kingdom
and the place that they'd have in it
when he did
their imaginations went wild
they could see themselves
seated on thrones
dressed in fancy robes
or
at banquet tables replete with meat and fine wine

these last few years walking in Jesus' company spoiled
them
they got used to
the welcoming shouts of enthusiastic crowds
the exciting conversations
the sensational miracles
the attention and respect they got from townspeople
wherever they went
what more could they ask of life
they wanted it to go on forever
and the one thing they didn't want to hear
was Jesus foretelling his death
and an end to the life they had grown accustomed to

one of the disciples poked Peter
as if to say
take Jesus aside and tell him

to stop talking like this
we know that is not going to happen to him
the people love him too much
to let the rulers crucify him
tell Jesus that he is the Messiah
and his future and ours
are destined to be glorious

Peter did what he was asked to do
and took Jesus aside and told him
what the others were saying behind his back
When he finished
Jesus turned immediately and in front of the disciples
rebuked Peter
"get behind me Satan
you are not thinking as God does
but as human beings do"

then to the crowd he said
"if you wish to follow me
forget yourselves
give the best you have to what you do
and seek nothing in return"

some in the crowd resented being called selfish
or as Jesus put it
"thinking as humans"
so they turned and walked away

but those thinking as God
trusted Jesus when he said
emptiness precedes fullness
and stayed by his side

the kingdom wasn't
what some might have thought it would be
fancy clothes and fine wine
but that didn't matter
for in their joy-filled hearts
there was no room for unhappiness

Jesus face to face

Unlike the two blind men at Jericho's gate
i had never met Jesus face to face
that is until today
Today i read their story again
but more attentively this time
standing close to Jesus listening
to his voice as he asked them
what it was they wished
Then i watched how intently he listened when they asked
 for sight
and freedom from the agony
of wondering what their friends meant when they said that
the moon is beautiful tonight or buds are appearing
on the tips of mulberry branches
Standing close i felt that he loved the blind men
as he loved himself and understood
their longing to live as fully as he does and others do
When the moment came for him to act
i watched as he approached the men to touch
and open their eyes saying as he did
 Let it be done according to your faith
At that very moment
i felt him touch my eyes
They opened
and unexpectedly i saw him face to face
No longer was he a miracle worker
living years ago
No longer was he a man to be studied
as though for an exam
He was a loving man standing as close to me
as he was to the blind men at Jericho's gate
and asked of me
 What is it that you wish
Without pausing i said
 To live with you this way always
Jesus said
 Let it be done to you according to your faith

Jesus listened

We hear from Jesus only once
between the time of his birth in Bethlehem
and his baptism by the Jordan River
And today is that time
Mary and Joseph
brought him at twelve years old
to Jerusalem to celebrate the Passover
When the celebration ended
his parents headed back home to Nazareth
thinking Jesus was following
They were wrong
He stayed in the temple asking
the teachers questions and listening to their answers
This is the first insight we get into the personality of Jesus
He listened to people
And it was this gift of listening intently
that set him apart from all others once he began
his ministry eighteen years later
It was then
immediately after his baptism by John
that he headed for the cities and towns of Palestine
and spent his time
listening to what people had to say

the mother who pleaded for the life of her son
the lepers who asked to be cleansed
the blind men who wanted to see as he saw
the man possessed by a demon who longed for freedom

or listening to the silence of those with nothing to say

the woman in the circle awaiting the executioners' stones
the man hiding in the corner of the synagogue ashamed to be seen
the poor people on the hillside hungry and far from home

the children laughing in the playground beside
Peter's home
the friendless tax collector squeezed between the
branches of the sycamore tree
Jesus listened in his lifetime here on earth
far more than he spoke
Little did the teachers in the temple
of Jerusalem anticipate that this young boy of twelve
sitting in their classroom
would grow up to change the world
by listening to people like you and me

Jesus was young and strong

Jesus was young and strong
when he stood in the center of the
synagogue in his town of Nazareth

he told his childhood friends
and their families
that he had come to preach
good news to the poor
open the eyes of the blind
set captives free

and he did what he said he would do
from one end of Palestine to the other
he did what he said he would do
never ceasing
always walking
talking to the crowds that followed his footsteps
healing and restoring hope

but his time here was short
what would have become of him
if he had lived beyond the age of thirty-three
what would he have done
if he lived to be as old as we
without the strength of thirty-three

he would have found a way
according to his age and strength
to bring hope to those
who thought that they had failed
sight to those who had stopped looking
freedom to those who had imprisoned
themselves in doubt

there is always work
for those within whom the spirit dwells
telling them to open their ears
to the cries of both men and beasts

Jesus within

Mary conceived the child
and as the child grew
she talked to him
as all mothers do
to the child within

on her way to Elizabeth's home
through the valley
and up the hill
to Ain Karim
she told him
of her dreams

the things they'd do
as he grew
--walks through the hills
--days by the sea
--hours in the workshop with his father

and as Mary talked
Jesus within listened
just as he does now
within us as we walk

learn to linger

A robin lingered on a spruce branch
just taking in the view.
Or was he listening for the sound of a worm?
Or for the sound of another robin?
No one knows for sure.
Robins keep to themselves.
They don't share their secrets.
They linger on branches until it is time to fly.
And my dog lingers, too.
He lingers by tree trunks and bushes.
Sometimes he just stares at them.
Other times he rivets his nose on their smells;
he is transfixed by them.
Nothing else in the world matters then;
he is in his own world and keeps its secrets to himself.

The bird and dog teach us to linger,
to slow down and pay attention to each second of time.
Not to rush through it, for it is full of everything we'll ever
need to know.

lepers walking as fast as they could

At the village gate of a small Galilean town
ten lepers met Jesus
and asked to be cleansed
Doesn't that sound so matter of fact
A lifetime of being ridiculed and shunned
and then a chance meeting and
a simple request for healing
It all seemed so
oh, by the way
Then without breaking his stride Jesus said
Go show yourselves to the priests
The lepers didn't waste a minute
They walked as fast as they could to the local synagogue
For years they had been sitting around
with nothing to talk about
but the miserable fate that had been dealt them
During the day
they sat by the town's gate
begging for food and pennies
During the night
they wrestled with nightmares
Years had gone by without
a decent meal
a hug or a laugh
They might as well have been dead
But then this moment
this mystery of being in the right place at the right
time
Go to the priests for a verdict of cleanliness
They who had been doing nothing for years
bandaged feet and hands
smelly bodies
frightful faces
asked to go as fast as they could
to the priests

They could hardly walk
But the very thought of cleanliness
    pulled them to their feet
    with a force they only knew when young
    and they headed for the synagogue
    with an anticipation that swallowed time
At least we know for sure that one made it
In a dramatic scene
    that one returned to Jesus
    fell to his knees
    knees that hadn't bent in years
    suddenly bent in thanksgiving
    what a scene
Jesus asked a question
    Where are the others
The leper shrugged his shoulders
He didn't know where the others were
He didn't offer any apologies
He left it up to Jesus to figure that out
Jesus changed the subject
He told the cleansed man to stand up on his own two feet
    to keep his head high
    to laugh for no good reason
    to go home and change his shirt
    for he had been saved
    and was free to dream again

a living presence

Jesus had an expression on his
face which we have all seen
at one time or another

it is an expression
which precedes words
we don't want to hear

we hoped
no prayed
that something would happen
that would have him change his mind

but nothing did
he told us that he was leaving
and we'd be on our own

each of us heard the words
in a different way
my world collapsed

i had gotten into the habit
of beginning each day
knowing he would make it work

that somehow some way
i wouldn't have to grope for joy
he would hand it to me

he would say things
about lilies making robes
finer than those worn by kings and queens

in my lifetime i had never met anyone like him
he seemed to come out of nowhere

with no introduction just an invitation

it was as simple as
come follow me
and like a fool i did

but i have learned since then
that love makes fools of all who
wish to take the chance

it was the chance
i wished to take
and now i've learned the price

he is leaving me on my own
i have become who i'd
never thought that i'd be

i owe it all to him
but now he's off
and i am left behind

before he goes
he takes my hand and says
what i'm sure he'll say to others

think of me not
as someone in your past but
as a living presence

ever at your side and
as close to you always
as i am now

never empty my words

of sound
but hear them as

being spoken
as fully as
at this very moment

because i love you
i know who you are
and who you are yet to be

so use what you have
don't save anything for later
give it now

later is an illusion
now is what matters
if not now it will never be

with my hand still in his
he says *courage*
it will be all right

once before i trusted him when
he said
come follow me

i did and have
loved each moment
so i trust him now

when he says
i will be with you always
now and forevermore

love others together

at the wedding reception in Cana
after Jesus had changed twelve jugs of water
into extraordinary wine
the newly married couple
knowing that they'd never meet another man like him
asked

> what can we do to ensure that our
> love for each other will last forever

Jesus said

> love others together

the man who could read the sea

Peter grew up as a fisherman's son.
His days began and ended on the water.
He learned everything
    there was to know about the sea
    from his father.
Jesus grew up the son of a carpenter.
From him he learned about hammers and saws
    and everything there
    was to know about tables and chairs
    but probably nothing about the sea.
It's no wonder that Peter balked
    when Jesus uninvited got into his boat
    and told him to put out
    into the deep waters and drop his nets.
But despite his balk
    he did as Jesus said
    and in minutes the nets were
    full of tilapia and whitefish.
Never had he made a catch like this.
No one had ever made a catch like this.
He'd be the talk of Capernaum
    and labeled a rich man.
Jesus however had another idea.
I want you to leave the nets here on the seashore
    and follow me.
Forget about the money you could have made
    and begin thinking about hillsides
    covered with people anxious to hear
    that there is more to life
    than nets tables and chairs.

Peter had a decision to make
tilapia at seven ninety-nine a pound
and whitefish at six
or following a man
he hardly knew
who could read the sea.
That thought scared the life out of him.
He fell to his knees.

a man with a shopping cart

Several times this week I've passed a man
pushing a shopping cart through the park
to the portable toilets next to the Carousel.
He didn't acknowledge my greetings.
He never took his eyes off the cart.
The black plastic bags stuffed into the cart
held everything he owned.
When he got to the "Royal Flush" he took the bags in
with him.
He didn't want them stolen.
They held everything he owned.
In one of them there was a blue shirt
which had been given to him on his birthday
many years ago.

Mark said what he had to say

Mark said what he had to say
in as few words as possible

he told the story of Jesus
in the shortest of the gospels

and he wrote it in such a way
that the story left us wanting more

whatever happened to the farmer
who lost a herd of swine

did he buy another herd
or had he had it with swine

and did he ever forgive Jesus
for sending his pigs over the cliff

and how about the blind man
who saw people looking like trees walking

what did he think
when he saw his wife for the first time

Mark was always in search of the words
to bring Jesus alive

to make him real and loveable
to involve him in our lives

and so it has been for centuries
everyone who has ever loved Jesus

has been seeking the words
to make Jesus' story

so attractive that
you want to meet him for yourself

Mary had questions

Mary was young but not naive
She lived in a house without doors
Her parents slept together
Her relatives
when they came to visit
did too
She knew about married life
She was committed to a man named Joseph
and dreamed of being with him soon
to start a family

So when Gabriel intruded
into her quiet life
and told her that she would conceive
and bear a son
she had questions
Mary was troubled but not cowed
She held her ground
and asked
    How can this be
    I have no relations with a man
Mary wanted answers
before she agreed to anything
no matter how sublime it sounded
I assume that the One who sent Gabriel
was listening in on the conversation
and was impressed by
Mary's self-confidence
and said when it ended
    That's the woman
    I want to be the mother
    of my son

meek and mild and angry

It was a sight to see
Jesus angry enough
to shout and swing a whip
His friends had never seen
him act that way before
Ordinarily he was calm
and soft-spoken
But today the temple packed with greedy merchants
selling doves and changing money
enraged him terribly
A horde of raging bulls
would fail to compare in kind
to his anger with their sacrilege
Holy ground
is meant for prayer and worship
not for merchandizing
Jesus left no doubt that
when we step on holy ground
it is to be with feet washed clean of greed and
selfishness
So if we wish to never see
the swirling whip of our shouting Lord
we ought remove our shoes and check our feet
before we step on holy ground

minding his business

Paul was on his way to Damascus
minding his business.
And his business was
getting rid of Christians.
He didn't like those who listened to Jesus
so he hunted them down
and put them in prison.
He was doing well
what he liked doing best.
But The Lord
had a different plan.
On his way to Damascus
Paul got knocked from his horse
and a voice from out of nowhere
told him to knock it off
for what he did to any one
no matter how wealthy or poor
he was doing to him.
And the "him" was Jesus
so Paul had better spend some time
in darkness and silence
thinking about his life.
And as always in silence and darkness
unexpected words and ideas came.
Sure enough Paul decided
that there were better things to do with his life
than enchain people
and drag them off to dungeons
so he stepped out into the sunlight
and walked from city to town to country
preaching the message of Jesus--
forget rituals and sacrifices
and unrelentingly practice compassion
love and forgiveness . . . these are the things that
matter.

miracles simple or spectacular

i don't expect
neighbors to perform
miracles

you know what i mean
taking a jug of water
and changing it into wine

but miracles
don't have to be
spectacular

simple is good
enough to qualify
for a miraculous definition

"open your eyes"
my neighbors said as i left
for the park this morning

"and notice the shining lampposts
standing upside down on the
black walnut surface of the pond"

for whatever reason my neighbors sensed
my imagination
was in need of resurrection

and as soon as
i saw the lampposts on the pond
it came alive

left the tomb
and it hasn't
stopped dancing since

the morning after the jazz festival

last night's jazz festival was a success
thousands came
the concession booths are still up
napkins cups and empty cans
are all over the place
a squirrel halfway up the trunk of an oak tree
is staring at me through one eye of a tilted head
another squirrel on the edge of a trash barrel
is watching every move i make
a robin perched on a cypress limb is doing the same
the squirrels and bird are thinking
ah for the time when we had the trees and fields
the worms and nuts all to ourselves
no humans sticking their noses into our dining room
ah the good ole days
but on the other hand
there were some birds and squirrels thinking
that if it weren't for humans
we wouldn't have popcorn and french fries

a mosaic beautiful to behold

I met Tony again this morning.
I've met him often over the past four years.
He was on his way to Union Station to catch a train for
Boston.
When the Red Sox are at home he goes to Fenway.
He doesn't miss a game.
He had on a sports jacket, shirt and tie, cap and, of course,
red socks.
I wished him a win.

When he crossed Gold Street and headed for the station,
Rich, another morning friend, came by.
He was on his way to the Gold Building.
He's a security guard there and starts at seven.
I told him about my meetings with Tony.
"O, yes," and then he told me that Tony is a fixture in
Hartford.
Everyone knows him.
Back in the seventies, he was a courier for the offices
downtown
and then as now a Red Sox fanatic.

Much of the joy in life is about putting
little pieces of it together.
A person here and a person there,
a word here and a word there
and before you know it
a mosaic develops,
a beautiful mosaic to behold.

my grandfather's Bible

here by my chair
on the top of a bookcase
is my grandfather's Bible
between brass Airedale bookends

as a child
i stayed with my grandparents
on the nights my parents
went to the dances at lake compounce
or to visit friends

my most vivid memory
of those overnights was
watching my grandfather end and begin
his days reading from this Bible

he would sit
on a straight back chair
next to the kitchen table
and read quietly

the faith with which he read
translated the scriptures unfailingly
into gentle words
and simple deeds

he wasn't aware of it
but he taught me more
than anything i had learned
in class or from the pulpit

nathanael

the fig tree
with its big leaves and stretching branches
was the best protection
from the scorching palestinian sun

nathanael sought its shade
not only for its coolness
but for the solitude it granted
and its prayerful invitation

his time beneath the fig tree
transformed nathanael
he became transparent
prayer and solitude will do that

it was just as nathanael
stepped out into the sun
that Jesus passing by
saw right through him

without hesitation
Jesus said
"here is a true child of israel
there is no duplicity in him"

immediately nathanael
became a disciple of Jesus
and while we don't know for sure
whether his name was nathanael or bartholomew

we do know this
that if we wish to be disciples of Jesus
the transparency afforded by prayer and solitude
is the best preparation

on God's time

The home of Jesus is filled today
with his friends
people like you and me
who loved and followed him
At the door will be those who have been waiting for us to come
those who loved us uniquely and taught us all that mattered
But there will be others there
those we had never met
but who taught us too what mattered
E. E. Cummings
taught us to look carefully at God's amazing world
and to watch for leaping trees and
to be on the lookout for clowns that hand out daisies
Therese
made it clear that the extraordinary side of holiness
has to do with doing the tiniest of things knowingly
G. K. Chesterton
said that if we were to walk along with Jesus
we'd need a sense of humor and be ready to laugh out loud
It will be delightful to meet these three face to face
and thank them for introducing us to a Jesus that wasn't plastic
And there are so many other introductions to be made
but there is no rush for we'll be on God's time then

on leavings

on leaving the park this morning
i knew i'd miss the
clouds trees grass
sound of the fountains' falling waters
sudden flight of doves
wave from trevor on his way to his bench
horn blow of devon's truck
fourteen ducks diving into the pond
silent buildings standing tall
hiss of buses pulling up gold street
solitary plane heading south
dome gleam flag
chance greetings of strangers and friends
flowers by the fox entrance
every leaving is final
i'll never return to that moment
every impression of it is compressed
and locked into it
when my memory unlocks it
in the future
i'll find that all the pieces
have been rearranged

one by one

Jesus stopped in capernaum
on his journey through palestine
the sick in huge numbers
were brought to him
and Jesus laid his hands
on each of them one by one
teaching by his manner
that it is the human touch that matters

the people of the town
begged him to stay with them
for there was much to do
but he said
"i have to move on
to the other towns of palestine
to teach there what i taught here--
that a crowd ceases to be a crowd
when you look into the eyes of each one
and see your own"

one finger

this morning i heard
thirty thousand feet
pounding out the message
in the park
don't forget
don't forget
one person's madness
can end
a child's laughter
and one child's laugh
is enough
to dispel
the sadness
of a crowd

now multiply that one
by twenty

the artist caught the moment
of God's finger
touching Adam's
freeing him
to explore
the mysteries of creation
that lie beyond the stars
beneath the surface of the seas
and everything in between

or . . .

our hands

In the beginning
with the touch of God's hand
we became who we are
God then sent us into the world
to reveal with our hands
the beauty of creation
With our hands we turn soil
and lay within it
tiny seeds
With our hands we tend the ground
carefully each day
until a garden's born
Within our hand a pen married to fantasy
can read minds and hearts
and unravel stories that never end
Within our hand
a brush can touch
a paint-laden palette
and arrange its reds yellows and blues
in shapes upon a canvas ready to
startle our imaginations
With our hands' nimble fingers
we can draw from strings
the sounds of seas and winds
With our hands we can fashion spires
that pierce the skies
and point us to eternity
With our hands we can find
within a piece of stone
the face of tranquility
With the touch of our hands
we can discover the beauty
deep within the one we love
God dwells within our hands
and through our hands
continually reveals the glories of creation

poetry is

over a cup of coffee
one quiet morning
i wrote a short poem

poetry is

a verbal photograph
a snapshot in words
a bird seen on a walk
a moment of awareness
an invitation to look
a journal in verse
a response to "Behold"
an album of verbal pictures
a journey's record
a "Grandma Moses" in words
a sketch in black ink
a watercolour painting
an observation wrapped in simple words
a record of what we think
a discipline of alertness
a recipe for contentment
a stepping stone to holiness
a way of life

prepare for The Lord

I met with John the Baptist last week
  to talk about this talk
Despite having just left the desert
  where he lived in solitude for years
  he was ready to talk
He wasn't in any way
  what I had
  expected him to be--
  grouchy and angry with the world
I told him that I had heard him say
  that we were to prepare ourselves
  for the coming of the Lord
  by straightening the highways
  and flattening the hills
  but i wasn't equipped to do that
He chuckled
That surprised me
He said that there were other
ways to prepare

The quizzical look on my face
  got him to answer

Be aware
  he said
when you awake each morning
pause for a moment
to thank God for the newest day of your life
and resolve to use it to its fullest

Be aware
  he said
when you walk down the ordinary
walkways of your life
to look carefully at the things

you have seen many times but never really noticed--
the dancing architecture of trees free of leaves

Be aware
he said
attend to the familiar voices of your life
you may have listened to the sounds of words
but didn't hear their meanings tucked beneath

Be aware
he said
watch where your feet go
for they will tell you who you are
more truthfully than another can

Be aware
he said
no two lives are alike
envy alone makes them the same

Be aware
he said
that the music matters
but the courage to dance the dance matters more

So when the day comes to meet the lord
he said
you can say that you didn't straighten any highways
or level any hills
but you were aware of the life you've lived
and that should be enough to win his love

psalm ninety -- mayflies

the mayflies by the pond
were after me this morning
    it's their time of year

they were in my eyes ears and nose
i swung my baseball cap
    in front of my face

hoping to fend them off
a vain defense
    they kept coming

a couple of them bit me on the ear
and another nipped my left eyelid
    they are relentless

they are renowned for their persistence
they have only so long to do what they came to do
    eat and reproduce

of all God's creatures
their life span is the shortest--
    one day

they can't waste a minute
they have so much to do
    and so little time

for the mayfly
there is no tomorrow
    literally

psalm ninety-eight

these two lines from psalm ninety-eight
walked with me this morning

" the rivers clap their hands
and the hills ring out their joy"

the psalmist
heard the waves of the rushing
rivers clapping their hands
as they jumped over boulders and stones
and the hills in the distance
laughing out loud as the wind
tussled the leaves of every tree
the waves clapped and the hills laughed
because everyone everywhere got to choose
what he or she wanted for breakfast

saints all around

Here the candles call us to be what we'll be
We sit with storied windows
outstretched hands
and a table to be filled
And we know as anything we have ever known
that others sat where we now sit and they have
gone
They are no longer here with hands to hold
or voices able to be heard
at least by hands or ears named ours
From this wood and glass and wax they have left
and gone to where they will live
more fully than here they ever did
Could it be the life they lived with us
so full of moments cherished
was only the beginning of who they are
Did the one who touched their dust and gave it life
intend it to be a thing that stayed beyond their
earthly time
Indeed
for silent words still come
transforming days and hours as before
but *now* in quite a different way
The ones we loved and who loved and taught us
who we have become are near us now
in ways not made by memory alone
It is more real now than when they sat as close as space
allowed
and in this saintly union we hear them speak as
now
and not as then
for the language that they speak is one we have
never heard
it comes and goes in silence
stirring self's soul to discover ones we thought we
knew
but had just begun

save from shame

Cana was a town of three hundred people in the hills of
Galilee
where weddings were community festivals
All the townspeople young and old
would come together for days to sing and dance
eat and drink in celebration of the marriage
of a couple they had watched grow from childhood
But midway through this festival
the wine ran out
Mary fearing the embarrassment
the bride and groom would have to bear
in a small town with a long memory
said to her son
They have no wine
Jesus said that this was not the time
to begin the work the Father sent him to do
But Mary thought differently--
love dictates the time
Then Jesus asked the waiters to bring him
the six water jugs standing by the door
They did and he touched the water within and
it instantly became extravagantly good red wine
more than enough to reach the end
of the festival and allow the
bride and groom to rejoice in their love
uninterrupted

Jesus might not have thought
that a hall
full of people celebrating young love
with dance song and good red wine
was the right time
to begin his Father's work
but looking back he realized it could not have begun
at a better time

scugnizzi

Every once in a while a word comes along that I like.
Solitude is one of them.
It's got a smooth rhythm to it:
So-li-tu-de.
Its sound invites me
To sit back, relax and think quietly.

I accept the invitation
And enter the room where I sit and write
Surrounded by the things
Of my life.

On the top of the bookshelf next to my chair
Is a brass statue of a young boy
That my father brought back to me as a gift
From Italy in nineteen-forty-five.

The boy has curly hair,
A tilted cap on the side of his head,
A cigarette butt hanging from his lips
And a defiant rise to his chin.

He was one of the "scugnizzi," my father said,
The name given boys who hung
Around the streets during the war
Begging for coins and cigarettes.

The "scugnizzi" had to look tough.
They had to survive the war
And were determined to survive
The embarrassment of begging.

Back seventy-four years ago
The defiant chin and cigarette butt
Gave the look he needed
To hide the fear inside.

Now in the solitude of my room
When he no longer has anything to fear
How would he dress
If given the chance to change his clothes?

Sea of Galilee

Jesus met his first followers
on the shore of Galilee's sea
they were fishermen
hauling in nets
and he asked them
to leave the nets
and follow him
to where they didn't know
or why they hadn't the slightest idea

but once they started
walking with him
things happened quickly
a jug of water turned to wine
a wild storm stood still
a thief shinnied up a tree and came down honest
a crippled lady saw the sky for the first time
a leper threw his bell away
and six elders had second thoughts about throwing stones
the followers realized
that they were
in the company of
an astonishing man

the three years in his company
traveling throughout Palestine
passed fast but the memories
of each day lingered
vivid memories of
a hillside of people anxious to hear him speak of peace
a young girl thought dead rising from her bed
and
the shouts of kingship
from an exuberant mob
as he rode into Jerusalem

on a donkey's back
had them dreaming of a kingdom
that soon might be theirs

but then
on a dark Thursday evening
after supper
a trusted friend's betrayal
shattered their dreams
Jesus was taken
beaten and hanged upon a cross
what had begun
so happily three years before in Cana
ended terribly on Golgotha

and with that
their journey with Jesus ended abruptly
for them there would be no more tomorrows
no more crowds
no more dreams
so they returned to the Sea of Galilee
to cast again their nets
as they had been raised to do
it was as though they had forgotten
the crowds on the hillsides
and the deaf man
who smiled when first he heard birds sing
they were ready to get on with their lives
until . . . on the seashore stood someone
they didn't recognize
that is
until he spoke

> Come with me and have breakfast
> a new day is about to begin
> now it is time for you

to set your own footsteps
perform your own miracles
it is for this moment
that I called you
from the shores of Galilee

a seed grows mysteriously

The seed grows mysteriously.
Watered by rain
nurtured by sun
a sprout breaks through
the surface of the soil
and defines itself
first a bud
then a flower.

What is even more mysterious
is how different
a bud is from a flower
which is full of colorful petals
spread like the wings
of finches.

And as seeds are to soil
words are to souls.
The lyrics of a song
the lines of a poem
the comments of a friend
all take root within the spirit
and grow to be far more
than could have been imagined
at first hearing.

Visit your garden today.
Walk slowly through the flowers
and recall the words cast
upon your soul
from a song
a poem
a friend
that have grown
to be things of beauty.

Rejoice and be glad
that you watered those words
from wherever they came
with desire
and nurtured them with care
for what could have been
a barren field
in the space of your life
is flush now with the scent of jonquils
and the dance of golden birds.

the shepherd and me

in Ezekiel:

I am one of a flock
that scatters at the sound of thunder
as pieces of dropped glass

the shepherd finds all the pieces
mends us together
and leads us to the mountain heights

where we can rest
and graze again
in rich pastures

in Psalm 23

I am a sheep
led by the shepherd
bringing me to a verdant pasture

where I refresh myself
by slow moving waters
murmuring a lullaby

and if it turns dark
I don't panic
for he never leaves my side

in the Gospel

I am a sheep who wanders from the flock
of a hundred sheep
and gets lost in the prickly shrubs

the shepherd misses me

he foolishly leaves the ninety-nine
and comes in search of me

he risks losing all for the sake of me
now tell me
do I mean that much to him

the son of Timaeus was a blind beggar

The son of Timaeus was a blind beggar
He sat alone on the same corner day after day
hoping that a passerby would drop a coin
into the drape of his cloak spread over his legs
Like most beggars he was nameless and invisible

But today something different was about to happen
He was blind but not deaf
He could hear the crowd shouting the name Jesus
A name he had heard before
the name of a miracle man

If Jesus can free others to talk and hear
he can free me to see
He sensed the crowd was getting close
He could feel the thump of their feet passing by
No one spoke to him
He wanted them to speak
but they rarely did
They were thinking of themselves
A terrible fear came over him
Jesus too was going to pass without a word
He was no different from all the rest

But the son of Timaeus leaped to his feet
flung off his cloak wildly as though to shed his shame
and began to shout at the top of his lungs
Jesus Jesus Jesus
speak to me
speak to me

Jesus heard his shouts turned and looked into his blinded
eyes
eyes that had never seen the sun rise
and asked

What is it that you wish
The beggar blurted out
I wish to see
I wish to see what you see
I wish to walk through water
and see what water looks like
to touch the leaves of trees and see what people
mean
when they say they're turning red
I wish to see as you see Jesus . . .
don't you understand

Jesus paused . . . wondering . . . finally

I do understand Bartimaeus
Now open your eyes
to see as i see
but know that you will see many things
that others may not

a speck of dust

while walking this morning
a gust of wind blew a speck of
dust into the corner
of my eye

with my fingertip
i took it out for examination
a mote is what it was
and from a dot of matter
not unlike what
i held within my hand
we became
what we are today
when touched by
the hand of God

the tenant and the owner

the preacher spoke so often of God
he believed he spoke for Him

and when corrected
he punished the critic

a title often
becomes an entitlement

the last state
of corruption

the only solution
is to kill the critic

and bury him
outside the vineyard walls

of this we can be sure--
          this echo of history rumbles on

the terribly bent woman

While teaching in the synagogue
Jesus saw a woman
off to the side of the room
who had been crippled for years
She was terribly bent over with her eyes fastened on the
    floor
She lived her life that way
passing everything as unnoticed
The moment to change that came
Jesus approached and told her to stand up straight
She did
She saw faces and eyes
and trembled at the revelation

The synagogue's official confronted Jesus
    It is the sabbath
    You have no right to cure today
Looking at the eyes of the official
Jesus said
    The moment of freedom
    doesn't know the day
    and it alone speaks for God
The woman stood still for a while before speaking
and then told Jesus the things she saw
things she hadn't noticed
the moving shadows on the wall flickering candles
    multicolored shawls
and faces that went with voices
Jesus listened and smiled
    Notice everything for nothing is inconsequential
    The treasury of freedom is filled with
        inconsequential things
The woman left the synagogue shameless and stared up
    at the sky

this morning at six-thirty

this morning at six thirty
i saw a young girl
perhaps in her twenties
looking up and down the big oak tree
which stands close by the
the pond in the park

as ramsey and i walked by
she pointed to the tree
and asked if i knew what
kind of a tree it was

i said it was a turkey oak
which has lived here in the park
for about a hundred and sixty years
and that there was another one like it
down by the carousel

she said that it is so beautiful
and so big
and that she loves it
and is sure that
the squirrels love it too

today is a day you won't forget

"Today is a day you won't forget.
I want you to choose a walking partner
from among your friends
and go into the towns and cities around here
and talk about the things that I've been talking about for
the past few years.

You know the things that I've talked about:
forgiving those who have cheated you,
feeding those who need to be fed,
walking slowly to catch the song of a bird,
treating yourself as kindly as you treat others,
and measuring your generosity with the largest cup
you have.

You are thinking that you can't remember everything
I said.
But if you can't remember everything,
think about the things you remember most about me and
talk about those things:
the morning I took the little girl's hand and told her to arise;
and how her parents' eyes teared when she stood;
the joyous yell the leper let out when I told him to go
home to his family;
the anger on the faces of the crowd when I said that
only the innocent could throw stones at the woman
in the circle.

You think that I am different and can do things you
can't do.
Nonsense.
You'll be surprised by what you can do with kindness and
mercy.
With gentle words and deeds you can resurrect life and
restore hope.

How does that differ from what I've done?
It's hard to accept this but hear me:
after I die, my life can go on only through you and those
who hear your words and witness your lives.

If you falter I falter,
so walk alongside someone you trust.
Bring no money,
no food, one pair of shoes, one jacket,
and a walking stick.
If you love me,
you'll have more than enough to do what I did.
Don't be afraid. You'll do remarkable things."

the trees are bare

bare trees
        crunchy snow
                hard ground
spent grass
        frozen pond
                closed rink
lonely elms
        vacant benches
                quieted fountains
absent ducks
        hidden moon
                earlier sun
grayish skies
        nasty winds
                temperamental temperatures

Rams is walking slowly
sniffing every fallen branch
while i--despite all this--suspect the park
is aware
        that winter is losing its grip
        that trees are talking about budding
        that geese are starting to head north
        that carousel horses are chomping at their bits
        that playground frogs are ready to spout
        that children are anxious to run barefoot in the hog
                river
        that benches are looking for company
        and the grass is itching to grow

this inexhaustible fascination with the things
        of heaven and earth is another definition of prayer

try as he may

when Jesus returned to the Father
he tried to tell him about
the life he had lived
here with us

he wanted to describe in detail
what it was like to live
as a man taking each day
as it came

but the words couldn't
keep up with the thirty-three years
of memories that
wanted his attention

he had to pick
the first one that came to mind
and describe it as well
as he could

it was his memory of
meeting Peter and Andrew
James and John
on the shore of the Galilean Sea

and how they trusted him enough at first glance
to pull in their boats
fold their nets and follow him
just for the asking

how could he possibly express
the thrill of being accepted by
people who hadn't the slightest
idea of who he was

from the moment he had been sent by the Father
into the world to teach
he wondered if anyone would care
or stop long enough to listen to what he had to say

but in that single split of a second
when strangers trusted the look of his face
and the sound of his voice without question
he knew that his mission had begun

the turkey oak by the carousel

they tell me that
the turkey oak standing by the carousel
in Bushnell Park is a hundred and fifty years old

i asked it
as i passed by it this morning
if it felt old

i haven't had time
to think about it
it said

twenty children

From the mountain top
the Lord looked down
upon the darkened valley of tears
and the river rushing through it
and called the sun
from behind the heavy clouds
and had it shine upon the rushing river
leaving brilliant sparkles
on the tip of every wave
It did as it was told and multiplied the sparkles
until lifted up by an inspirited wind
they merged at the mountaintop
into an overwhelming brilliance
dispelling the darkness below
and spreading light from mountaintop to mountain
until distance lost its meaning
and valleys were no longer dark

the vain moon

the vain moon
dodges
the clouds

the robin
sings his side
of loneliness

the old woman
washes her hands
on the morning leaves

eyes shut
the fountain
applauds

the crow broken
struggles
beneath the bush

Venus the thief

Today Venus passes between the earth and the sun.
All that we'll be able to see from here is a black dot on the
sun's face.
Three thousand years from today, poets will be looking for
something exceptional
to say about the sun.
They'll spot on its face the small black dot and wonder
what it is.
One of them will recall having heard an ancient myth
about a beauty mark stolen by Venus from the face
of Marilyn Monroe, a gorgeous actress, while she
was sleeping.
Then Venus bestowed it as a gift on the cheek of
her lover Apollo
during one of their clandestine meetings.

Ah, myths. What would we do without them?

wealth willed to the awake

a walk beneath a clear sky
watching jupiter travel west
accompanied by the stars nath and bellatrix
and followed by venus the sun's escort into day
wills a wealth upon the awake
that defies any barn to hold

what's in a name

Back in the thirties and forties,
when I was growing up
and playing cops and robbers,
I didn't like my name Henry.
I wanted to be called Jim.
Cops are called Jim.
Jim is a short name.
Not like Henry: two syllables and by wise guys three.
Jim could be said quickly and forcefully.
Jim signals a rugged guy with things to do and
places to go.
But I had nothing to say about my name.

Neither did John.
The angel, Elizabeth and Zachariah
agreed the child's name was to be John.
But secretly, he called himself Zack.
A name short and to the point.
Zack, one syllable not four
befitting a man
who had things to do
and places to go.

When he got old enough
to take care of himself,
he headed for the desert
and decided to be a prophet,
the prophet sent into the world to prepare the
way of the Lord.

Out there with cactus and sand
and no one who knew him
he was Zack to himself until
the moment came for him to leave the desert
and do the thing he had been born to do--

level the mountains and fill the valleys.
Then he reverted to the name
given him by the angel, his mother and father: John.

He might not have liked it, but
it too was a short name, to the point, and implied
a man with plenty of things to do
and places to go.

will you also leave

The crowd that surrounded Jesus
on the shore of the Sea of Galilee
came to him expecting
to hear hopeful things and witness marvelous deeds.

Instead Jesus astounded them by saying,
"I am the living bread that has come down from heaven;
whoever eats this bread will live forever;
and the bread I give is my flesh for the life of the world."

This wasn't what the crowd came to hear.
They thought his words were extravagant
and they grumbled in disgust
and many turned and went back to their former way of life.

Then Jesus asked those still standing by his side,
"Do you also want to leave?"
Jesus asks the same of us now when we hear
him say, ". . . the bread I give is my flesh for the life of the
world."

Our presence is our answer.
Here near to you, Lord, is where we wish to be
ready to reach out
and hold you in our hands.

And in that brief moment of holding
we wish not to be who we were
but who we want to be, Lord,
in the moments ahead.

Accordingly,
we set our footsteps in a new direction
anxious to see the world and our life within it
in a way we had not seen them before:

trusting we'll discover on our way
the talents we've kept concealed
for fear that their performance
would be covered with embarrassment,

believing that we'll find in your words
the strength to perfect
our fidelity and loyalty
to those entrusted to our care,

hoping that your closeness will inspire us
to seek the fulfilment of our fondest dreams--
being people of consistent kindness
and unbending generosity,

seeking the solitude needed to examine
the values that drive our lives
and the honesty to discard
those that dehumanize us.

There is no moment of faith more intense
than the one in which we reach out our hands to hold
the Body of the living Christ--
the life upon which our life depends.

In that tremendous moment
we no longer live
but Christ
lives in us.

Our hopes, dreams and deeds
become as his and we rejoice
that we didn't turn
our backs and walk away.

the wise ones

the wise ones tell us that
if we wish to know who we are
we must follow
our footsteps

begin at daybreak
and end with nightfall
watching where
our feet take us

keep simple notes
where we went
who we met
what we did

keep the notebook
clear and simple
observation is all that's needed
awareness gradually unfolds

and eventually we'll
discover who we are
and what our life
is all about

no one needs to tell us
self revelation
is inevitable
the wise ones say

words can be felt

words can be felt
we can feel Jesus being scourged
his hands tied above his head
his back bared
and a whip swung by a brute
swung repeatedly until
his skin swells and breaks
with every lash

words can be felt
the crown of thorns
mimicking the emblem of a king
is forced down upon his head
until the thorns bend upon his skull
and break though the tender flesh
above his eyes

words can be felt
Jesus robed in noble scarlet
in the custom of kings
and soldiers with nothing else to do
but what they were told to do
whack his face shouting
say now that you are a king
say again you are a king

words can be felt
the whips and thorns and blows
were torturous but nothing more so
than the excruciating pain of the betrayal
of one who had walked with him day by day
preaching the law of love

the world lent to me

Another one of the joys which
i'll hang on to
is this morning's walk though
the park
At six-thirty rams and i crossed
wells street and walked
between a row
of fourteen cherry trees
They were wrapped in small white lights
and soft snow
We crossed through the east field
layered in four inches of fresh snow
Rams had a ball running through the field
grabbing mouthfuls of snow shaking his head
smiling and barking at a tiny dog
running loose by the Horace Wells statue
All of the trees looked beautiful in white
but the spruce trees
stood out
Their branches were heavy with snow
and appeared to be carefully decorated
for an upcoming stage show
There was an unusual stillness to the park
at this hour
The sound of cars and buses was muffled
And I wasn't aware of horns blaring
Maybe drivers were concentrating on
dodging the slippery spots on the roads
Whatever
It was quiet out there this morning

I am so fortunate to live here and have rams
He gets me out every day
Left to myself
i'd probably never get out at six thirty

to walk through Bushnell Park alone
But rams does it to me every morning
at about the same time
He gets me to enjoy the snow
the sound of nothing
the stars and moon
when they are out and the changing sky
He forces me to notice the lampposts
the trees trash barrels and park benches
No doubt about it
He is God sent
to keep me awake to the world
lent to me for a while

world right side up

Ezra and Eliakim were brothers
both were successful wheat farmers

Their fields and barns were on opposing sides of a hill
on the western countryside of Jerusalem

At harvest time they divided their fields' yield of wheat
equally and stored it in their barns thanking God for
his lavishness

Ezra had a wife and seven sons
Eliakim was single

One night Eliakim thought that Ezra with nine mouths to
feed could use some help

I have only myself to tend
i can get along with less

So each night Eliakim packed a bag of wheat
and carried it over the hill to Ezra's barn
and left it there

Ezra knew his brother was alone
and needed to be provided for his days of age

So he packed a bag of wheat every night and carried it
over the hill to Eliakim's barn and left it there

At daybreak when the brothers waked and entered their
barns each found his gift of wheat mysteriously
replaced

Both were dumbfounded
but never told the other of the nightly miracle

Then one night when the sky was clear
each set out for his brother's barn on the other
side of the hill

Their pace to the top was happily matched
and they met by chance midway between the barns

At first sight they cried and then they laughed
and then were wrapped in each other's arms

No sooner done than the moon shone as brightly as the
sun and they could see beneath the hill on which
they stood

rows and rows of barren trees
sprouting tender leaves of green

telling them the love they shared
turned the world up-right

and became the world
its Creator wished that it would be . . . so very long
ago

you never come face-to-face with God

you never come face-to-face with God
instantly
you get a lot of glimpses of him
that you have to put together
with the other glimpses
you have caught
on your morning walk

the smile on the face
of a young girl walking her dog

a blue heron standing motionless
in the shallows of the pond

the sun gradually
taking control of the sky

a clump of trees
minding their own business

birds getting out
of one another's way

clouds following the same
route they took yesterday

when your walk is done
you can put all the glimpses together
and get the face of God

your unprecedented earthly life

think of your unprecedented earthly life
from the moment of welcoming hands
to the moment now unfolding as you
sit here among people who believe as you do
listening to the parable of the barren fig tree

in the parable
the owner of the tree
wanted the gardener to
cut it down
for it had borne
no fruit in three years

the gardener pleaded for the tree
asking for at least one more year
to prove that it would bear fruit
and the taste of its figs
would convince the owner that
it was worth the wait

see yourself standing in the crowd
listening to the parable and
apply it to yourself
you are the tree that has borne no fruit
and the owner wants you
chopped down

but the gardener begs the owner
to give you another chance
to stand in the sun
and feed on the riches of the soil
assuring him that you will bear abundant fruit

the owner honors the gardener's plea
now what will you do with this grant of time
will you use it
as never before

will you give your best
to your unprecedented earthly life
will you undo
what you dislike most
about what you see in your mirror
will you erase the point of no return
and write the opening sentence of
a brand new story
will you live as you wish to live
and not as the
world wishes you to

at harvest time
the gardener led the owner
to the orchard
stopped at the tree
plucked a fig
handed it to the owner
and said
        taste and see
        it was worth the wait
                    . . . . wasn't it

Zacchaeus

We were in Jerico yesterday
Recall that the streets were crowed then too
Jesus was there and the crowds wanted to be near him
Remember Bartimaeus kept shouting for attention
  Jesus
  let me see
  let me see
Jesus opened Bartimaeus' eyes and he saw inside and
  outside of himself
Today we are in Jerico again
Jesus is still there and the crowd still wants to be near him
One man in particular wants to be near him
But the crowd is too big and tall
But wily Zacchaeus outsmarts it
He runs ahead of the shouting crowd and climbs a tree
He sees Jesus
Jesus sees him and tells him to climb down
  and take him home
As told
  Zacchaeus shinnies down the Sycamore tree
  and invites Jesus into his house
  a big house reflecting his wealth
Zacchaeus is overwhelmed by the self-confidence of Jesus
Jesus doesn't care what people say about him
  that he dines with a tax collector
  a friend to no one in town
So overwhelmed by the brave love of Jesus for him
  that he shares his wealth time and table with the poor
Jesus says to him
  you are why I came
  to save you
  to set you free from what you thought was
    important
  things and coins

now go and live your life to the limit
keep your head high and others will think you are
taller than you are